published + edited by

asterios agkathidis
markus hudert
gabi schillig

form defining strategies
experimental architectural design

3d print, 2011

32 A<small>CKLMNS</small>
linear stratification

30 A<small>CKLMNS</small>
cross vaults

28 A<small>CKLMNS</small>
baked cocoon

24 A<small>CKLMNS</small>
perforated skin

22 A<small>CKLMNS</small>
profiles

20 A<small>CKLMNS</small>
tubular spine

18 A<small>CKLMNS</small>
textile moulds

16 A<small>CKLMNS</small>
spatial extrusion

60 K<small>ACLNMS</small>
textile operations

58 K<small>ACLNMS</small>
interlocking loops

54 K<small>ACLNMS</small>
woven garment

ACCUMULATION   **CONSTRAINT FOLDING**   **KNOTTING**   **LINEAR DYNAMICS**

46 C<small>AKLMNS</small>
soft triangles

48 C<small>AKLMNS</small>
multidirectional folding

50 C<small>AKLMNS</small>
folded wave

52 C<small>AKLMNS</small>
distorted mesh

76 L<small>ACKNMS</small>
spinal spin

78 L<small>ACKNMS</small>
(a)symmetry

82 L<small>ACKNMS</small>
cause and effect

84 L<small>ACKNMS</small>
linear surface

86 L<small>ACKNMS</small>
interwoven stripes

INTRODUCTION

This book examines experimental design methodologies in the field of architecture and their implementation in academic settings. Theoretical considerations by guest essayists and numerous examples of conceptual designs complement our holistic approach to the subject matter.

The studies collected here emerged during weekly workshops during 2007 and 2008 with architecture students at the Technische Universität Darmstadt[1] and the Aristotele University of Thessaloniki[2].

Usual designg parameters such as functional specifications and local context were not considered. The models that emerged are organizational systems that have been developed through diagrammatic thinking and are therefore capable of representing processed data and strategies.

The starting point of the teaching concept was a divergence from the usual methods and ways of thinking, allowing for new, innovative solutions to emerge during the design process. The development of novel spatial modules, in coherence with material and structural considerations, was actively encouraged.

During the workshop various design techniques were applied that enabled the development of integrative spatial concepts. Geometry played an essential role here.

Studies were later developed by following given rules, converting them into diagrams and then finally, and perhaps most importantly, through the use of physical models.

Thereby the question of materiality becomes a crucial consideration: the characteristics of different materials that were used for the models did not just influence geometrical possibilities, but brought with them material specific effects, with which spatial qualities could be intensified, explored and organised.

This methodology is based on our conviction that working with physical models is indispensable even in today's all-digital climate. Architects are able to explore unpredictable, unimagined, unexpected and exciting spatiality that can emerge organically during the design process. Novel, innovative spatial structures and systems are discovered and inform this process and subsequent decisions.

It becomes clear that the design process in architecture has to be understood as a conscious, sensible yet ambitious process to investigate and apply innovative notions of space to construction.

Asterios Agkathidis, Markus Hudert, Gabi Schillig, Frankfurt am Main, Fall 2011

1) Chair of EKON, Professor Moriz Hauschild
2) Studio "other places" Sasa Lada, Associate Professor & Aleka Alexopoulou, Assistant Professor

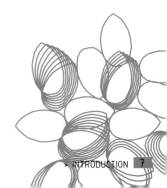

IN THE GARDEN OF FORM

by johan bettum

In an essay on thematic variation in central European literature, the Serbian writer, Danilo Kis, characterises *a deliberate use of literary form as a personal and political means in a series of endeavours* 1). Kis offers his view on literary form with the reservation that he might 'only be generalising from (his own) intellectual and literary obsessions.' Yet, his endeavours deserve attention, not only in light of the political turmoil of central Europe after the Second World War (in the 20th century, Serbia formed the core of various South Slavic states and declared its independence from the state union of Serbia and Montenegro in 2006), since they suggest that literary form may safeguard against the pandemonium of everything that is pointless, nonsensical and, quite simply, bad.

THE CRISIS OF ARCHITECTURAL FORM: „THAT IS NOT MY MOTHER"

As an architect, it is hard not to embrace the production of form. Even those who argue that contemporary architecture is not about form, present more of a classical Freudian negation ("that is not my mother") than a pervasive architectural point of view. One can argue about architectural form in different ways, but one always returns to it and the architect dreams of handing over more or less substantial and pervasive manifestations of it.

Kis writes: '*Were I to say that awareness of form is one of the common traits of central European writers - form as a desire to make sense of life and metaphysical ambiguities, form as the possibility of choice, form as an attempt to pinpoint an Archimedean fulcrum in the chaos surrounding us, form as the bulwark against the mayhem of barbarism and the irrational caprice of instinct...*'

KIS' MULTIVALENT FORM

Accepting the dangers of leaping disciplinary barriers and political contexts, the temptation to appropriate Kis' passage for architectural purposes is irresistible. In so doing, one cannot ignore the multivalence he invests in form. On one hand, form is leverage out of existential languish, fortification against the decay of culture and defence against the groundless whims of human nature. But, on the other hand, form also offers choice; and, in providing Archimedean stability in a sea of chaos, it forms a 'fulcrum', a pivot point or a hinge, around which we turn. Thus, Kis' multivalent literary form proffers two seemingly opposing forces, resulting respectively in rootedness and movement. The former works its ways against the pernicious ways of humanity; the latter gives the same humanity freedom and leeway to act.

But the question of architectural form has under-
gone a kind of crisis during the last two decades,
turning too many architects into something like
rash adolescents incapable of handling the enor-
mous questions implicit in a design problem. This
crisis stems in part from the incredible powers
of computers to generate just about any form,
depending on the parameters of the software
used. In this period, architecture has turned from
a programmatically or ideologically driven production of form (well exemplified by Modernism)
to a laissez-faire making of unmotivated form.
In some camps, this has led to an increasing
uneasiness and frustration with the contemporary
production of architectural form.

In the wake of any crisis, there are consequences
and responses. In addition to those who are hap-
py with the state of affairs, one gets the conservative and reactionary ("pull back and return to past
certainties"), the radical and daring ("push on
quickly and see what happens") and inquisitive
and probing ("what, why, how…"). Each camp
can produce good architecture, because, after
all, there is no prescription for that. But the latter
group, the inquisitive and probing, is most likely
to produce the next moment of release and further development – particularly since it pursues
and seeks to unravel the underlying structure of
what is at hand.

THE FULCRUM

In this context, Danilo Kis' notions of an Archimedean fulcrum emerge as highly evocative. Archimedes, the ancient Greek mathematician, physicist and engineer, discovered the principle of buoyancy and provided the first rigorous explanation of leverage. The fulcrum is the point on which a lever rests or is supported and on which it pivots; a fulcrum may play an essential role in an activity or event. Thus, the fulcrum is the point around which a movement takes place, something happens. In architectural terms, one can say that the space of a certain movement is formed around it. If one were to describe it, it consists of a point and a line, and the mere outline of these forms the backbone for the pivotal movement.

The majority of the models presented in this book can be thought of as analogous to the Archimedean fulcrum. They form the backbone of a possible form – or, more correctly, possible forms. Around them and even through them, forms can be derived in a continuous process of transformation. These forms would correspond to the space that "the fulcrum" implicitly describes.

The multiple possibilities of form that is inherent in each model, echoes with Kis' notion of the possibility of choice. Of course, choice is freedom and freedom is what we associate with a creative, liberated individual. In this sense, the models document everything that comes before form; they are the seeds from which architectural forms and, eventually, building proposals can be had. We are in the *Garden of Form*, 2) almost at the beginning, and we are looking at those things (like a rib) from which architecture may rise.

THE POLITICALLY CORRECT & THE FUTURE OF ARCHITECTURE

The less optimistic view would be that the models are all about architectural form and only that. In that case, the analysis above is void and the efforts set out in this book are more conservative than they would like to be. To most architects, the process of modelling has a teleological nature; the modelling process is merely there to expedite the architectural form. To argue something else is almost politically incorrect; almost completed, whole forms must be architectural forms, not a hinge to some other state of modelling.

But if one is truly interested in architectural form today, the questions of what, why and how are the only ones that may look ahead, out of the turmoil that computerised processes have created, and back to a situation where architects once more exert some level of control over the creative process. The context and implications of this go far beyond the modelling; implicit are also new forms of materiality, new systems of information that can be embedded in the architectural elements, new types of manufacture and construction, and new ways to tailor the architectural forms for specific types of performances – be they ecological, informational, merely structural, aesthetic or all of those.

Physical modelling is not the only medium for addressing these questions; in many places advanced digital processes are employed for the same purpose. But physical modelling retains its power to manifest and suggest relations, scales and forms of organisation that digital models often do only with difficulty. Not the least, physical models are more prone to chance and productive errors. For this reason, models that outline the possibility for form, models that are merely rib-like and suggestive, are also powerful since they require reading, necessitate interpretation and beg intervention. They are the springboard to architecture.

Whether architectural form can also withstand barbarism and the irrational caprice of instinct, is another question. In the age of digital tecnology, that may be at best left to literary form.

LITERATURE
1) Kis, 1996, Homo Poeticus: Essays and Interviews, 95-114 p.114. The essay was originally published in 1986.
2) The title is inspired by a book by Danilo Kis: Garden, Ashes.

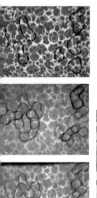

spatial extrusion

This project aims to achieve a spatial extrusion of the initial two-dimensional surface, which was inspired by the structure of metal foam. First, several sheets were layered on top of one another, then connected at chosen points while applying a horizontal shift at the same time. The horizontal displacements created vertical deformations. The material tension results in dynamic interstitial relationships and fluidity of space.

>TECHNIQUES cutting, folding, layering
>MATERIALS white and black cardboard

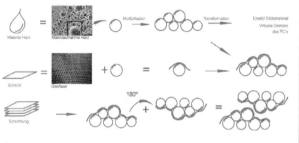 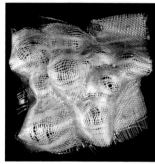

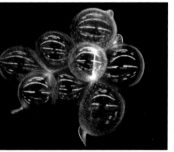  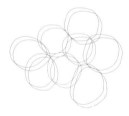

>TECHNIQUES pumping, wrapping, beating, liquefying
>MATERIAL glass fiber, resin, textile, PVC membrane

textile moulds

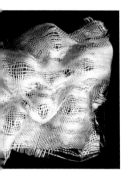

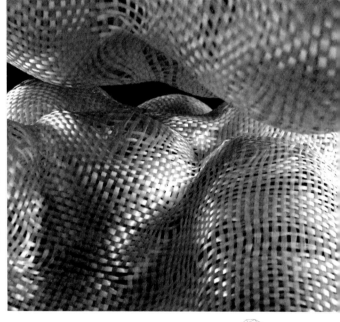

An agglomeration of spheres, varying in diameter, generates structural clusters. By introducing an additional enveloping technique, the emerging surface is trapped and fixed. It operates both as a skin and landscape.

tubular spine

A two-dimensional surface is transformed into a tubular space by applying a thermo-forming technique. The emerging geometry can be adjusted in order to accommodate modulations of its interior or exterior surface.

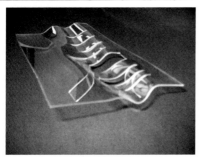 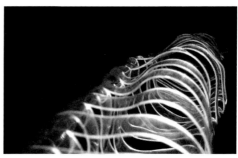

>TECHNIQUES cutting, weaving, thermoforming
>MATERIAL PVC sheet

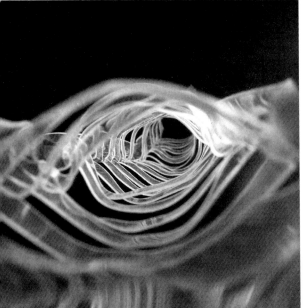

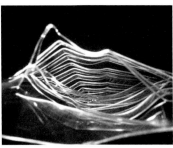

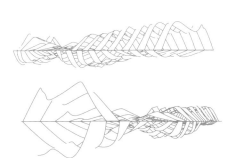

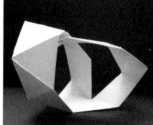

A three dimensional wave structure is the original form to which a linear folding technique is applied. The rounded geometry is being transformed into fractal like forms so it becomes possible to profile these. The emerging structure exhibits extreme contrasts between light and dark and open and closed spaces.

profiles

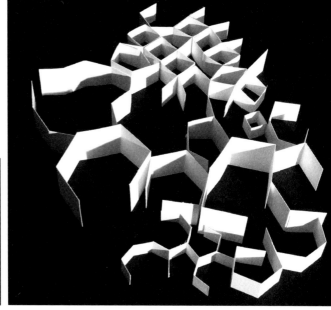

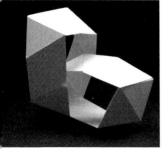

>TECHNIQUES contour crafting
>MATERIALS wood, paper, cardboard

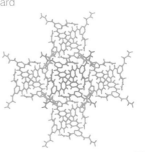

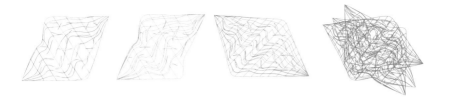

>TECHNIQUES cutting, bending, stretching, thermoforming, layering
>MATERIAL PVC foil

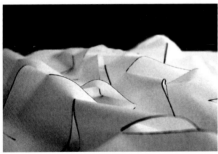

This model aims to explore spatial surface conditions. By using cutting and thermo-forming techniques, the two-dimensional surfaces deform to create a three dimensional structure.

Three additional layers are overlapped and rotated by 45°. The final product could be read as a spatial landscape or as an instrument for generating architecture.

perforated skin

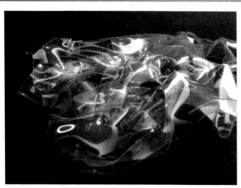

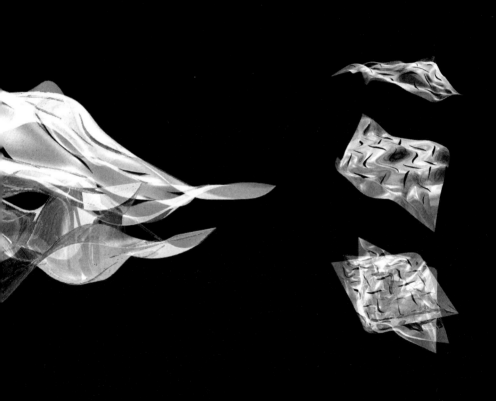

>TECHNIQUES cutting, bending, baking
>MATERIALS pvc sheets

A nerve cell structure is being applied on a double sheet of PVC. Each nodal point is being bound with each opposite side neighbor. The emerging object was literally being baked in the oven, thus it finally forms in its present cocoon shape.

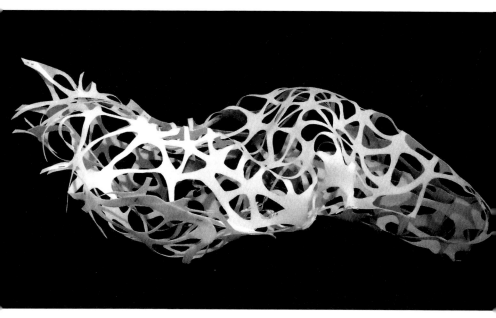

baked cocoon

cross vaults

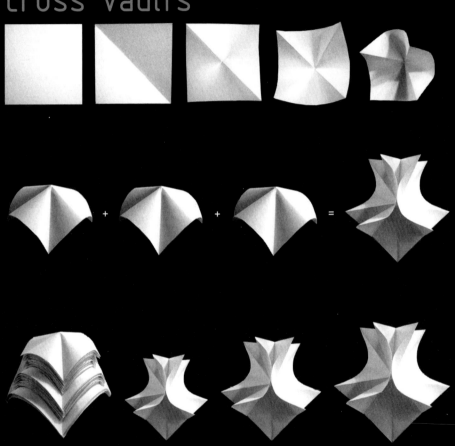

>TECHNIQUES folding
>MATERIALS paper

Peaces of paper were folded in cross vault formation, with differentiated span widths. The produced units were accumulated in clusters, allowing new geometrical constellations.

linear stratification

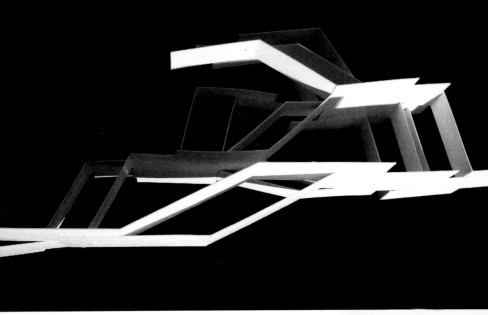

>TECHNIQUES folding, multiplying
>MATERIALS cardboard

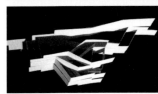

Two linear elements are joined into a linear-rhombic module which can perform at different angles. The embedded growing mechanism allows the addition of modules into a cluster which adopts all entities of the single unit: linear spatial transform-ability.

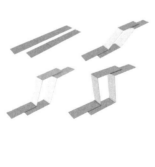

MODULARITY CHANGES

by asterios agkathidis

CONCEPTUAL DEFINITION
Modularity was first brought to our attention by Vitruvius. By analysing the "Doric order" present in the ancient Greek temples, he intro-duces the "module" (*modulus*)[1] as a minimum unit by which any other component of the temple may be measured. By applying the rule to the Parthenon, he explores further the 4 : 6 : 9 module to the other dimensions of the building, which he defines by the size of the "triglyph" (= 875.9mm). Thus, each structural element of the temple has a precisely defined relation to other elements and the rest of the building as a whole.

The notion of modularity has been known to European architecture and construction since the classical period. It can be described as a system which allows economy and efficiency in the design and realization of architectural projects. Nevertheless, modularity is not a static term, but a constantly shifting notion, which re-adjusts its meaning in relation to contemporary manufacturing and production technology, taking its lead from significant technological innovations.

By examining the Parthenon in terms of manufacturing, we can see that the temple shows many characteristics of contemporary building. It is constructed of standardised, modular pieces, which were manufactured to a high degree of precision under quasi industrial conditions. Considering this, modularity as defined in the classical period becomes a determination technique for

Today, in the midst of the digital and information revolutions, modularity seems to be undergoing a drastic realignment. CAD/CAM technologies have revolutionised the production of constructional elements, as much as design and form-defining mechanisms.

the parthenon

modular tiles, porto

design, organization and efficiency in construction. The "rhythm" of the ratio 4:6:9 functions as design tool and detailing principle at the same time. The module is not a physical element but a theoretical definition of a measurement, which operates as a form defining and problem-solving mechanism.

IDENTICAL UNITS

Modular constructions appear again in abundance as a consequence of colonial expansion and industrial revolution. The lack of skilled craftsmen in the new world forced engineers to develop light, modular constructions that would allow standardised mass production on an industrial scale and facilitate the easy assembly of the component pieces on site.

Thus, the first industrially produced construction system came into being: the balloon frame. Its name reflects its lightness and its "high-tech" construction, which was similar to the balloons, or the woven baskets.

The "*balloon frame*"[2] could be described as a technique based around structural units, called "studs", which provide a stable frame to which interior and exterior wall coverings were attached and covered by a roof comprising horizontal joists or sloping rafters covered by various sheathing materials.

The wooden frames become identical modules, which are being repeatedly added, generating a regular three-dimensional grid. Their width and height determined the dimensions of doors and windows, the stairs and roof. Thus a regular system of order arises, which in later stages expands even to an urban scale, through mass replication in the construction of housing units.

The "balloon frame construction" and the later optimised version, the "general panel system",describes a module as a physically identical unit, which is multiplied and repeated. The module is characterised by the greatest possible simplicity and its suitability for economical mass production. The building itself can also be seen as a unit, or a spatial module. This definition of modularity dominated architecture for many decades, with several variations in the modern, late and post modern period, always linked to the emergence of new manufacturing techniques and materials. Here, I could make reference to the modern movement with Walter Gropius´ "Baukastensystem", and the Metabolists.

modular „housing", bird fair, porto

PARAMETRIC SET

Today, the cultural and social revolution brought on by telecommunication and information technologies is rapidly transforming the field of architecture. We live in an era of accelerated change, in which data speeds invisibly around us, the flow of information superseding the importance of material exchange. Complex digital infrastructures have inscribed themselves within our well established mechanical and urban patterns. Today the unique character of handicraft and the industrial sameness of systematic mass production can coexist thanks to CAD/CAM, which assists the production of series manufactured, mathematically coherent but differentiated objects, as well as elaborate and relatively cheap one-off components.

Peter Zellner describes the transformation of architecture thus, *"Architecture is becoming like "firmware", the digital building of software space inscribed in the hardwares of construction. Soft, complex curved surfaces modelled in dataspace will be transmuted to real space as bent or tongued variable panels, as sheets in steel, copper or plastics, or as Kevlar or glass-fiber*

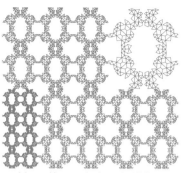

modular pattern, asterios agkathidis

skins; *massive involuted elements designed in data-space become milled, routed or turned elements in wood or alumi-nium, or cut as moulds for quick-setting resins, rubbers or metals. Bridging the boundaries between the real-technical and the virtual-technical, firmware will favour a far more malleable relationship between bits, space and matter."*[3]

In this spectrum of rapid transition, the understanding of modules as identical physical objects seems to be meaningless. Never before was the call for standardisation in a globalised world stronger than it is now. Could modularity today be defined as an parametric set that determines the variation of different elements?

Could modularity ever constitute a common set of rules by which any module can be determined? Is a module essential in order to allow control of the design process, production techniques and efficiency in construction?

LITERATURE
1.2001, Baukunst, 2 Bde. Bücher I - X, Marcus Vitruvius Pollio, Birkhäuser Verlag, Basel
2.1998, "Mobile Architektur", Ludwig Matthias, Deutsche Verlags-Anstalt DVA, Munich
3.1999, Hybrid Space / New Forms in Digital Architecture", Zellner Peter, Rizzoli International Publications, New York.

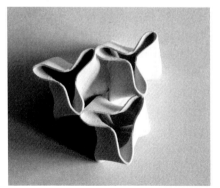

rapid prototype by Bernhardt Bangert

OPERATIVE SUBDIVISION

by markus hudert

THE FACETTED SURFACE

When the first artificial, manmade shelters were created, there were almost no planar building materials available. Apart from the usage of clay, homogeneous surfaces were as almost impossible to create. Therefore the sheltering surfaces needed to be assembled out of mostly linear elements. Archaeological research 1) brought to light that the first manmade structures dating back to 400.000 BC and located close to Nizza consisted of branches and leaves.

Apart from its role as interface between interior and exterior spaces, there are also the aspects of its texture and its articulation that make the surface a key element of architecture. Without the surface it is hard if not impossible to create and to capture what is essential to architecture: spatiality and representation. In former times architects took advantage of the necessity of assemblage and enriched purely functional aspects with decorative qualities. Also, the ancient builder fulfilled both the role of the architect and the role of engineer, two professions that are separated today. There was a better understanding of the limits and characteristics of each material. The planned buildings were appropriate to the material used.

The knowledge and application of the correlation between the surface as a whole on the one hand and the parts that built it up on the other was always paralleled by the wish to create seamless, continuous surfaces. This desire was fulfilled with the invention of reinforced concrete. But the process of the setting up of concrete structures also had disadvantages. Compared to the technologies of industrialisation that appeared almost at the same time, its production was achieved by rather primitive means. It was probably for this reason that architects like Konrad Wachsmann were promoting the method of assembly with modern means instead:

'...The term 'building' should be removed from the vocabulary and be replaced by a word that rather describes the term assemblage, the term of joining, meaning the art of joining or better 'The art of the join'. The organic, logic and systematic design will dominate.' 2)

As in former times, it remained critical for the successful application of assemblage to keep in mind the relation between the whole and its parts. Before the assemblage could take place in the building phase, the subdivision of the whole needed to be worked out during the planning stage.

SEPARATION OF KNOWLEDGE

It is hard to say when, but gradually this knowledge became of secondary importance and aspects of formal expression, aesthetics and conception became predominant. Most architects today are still thinking within these paradigms of the architectonic idea. A pattern of thinking and producing architecture, which, at a certain point of the process, makes a translation from the immaterial to the material obligatory. This attitude did not change when the technology of CAD was introduced to architecture.

The new visual and spatial possibilities of this technology created a huge euphoria, as they opened up a new dimension for the above named aspects of architecture. Today, more then ten years after this digital revolution in architecture, we have arrived at a point where the usage of the computer as a design tool needs to be re-thought. The computer allowed us to continue where the visions of modernist architects such as Frank Lloyd Wright had stopped. It allowed the creation of fascinating constructs of endless dynamic spaces, held together by complex continuous surfaces. Yet, many of these designs were and are lacking something. They remain digital artefacts, as they are created in the artificial, limitless world of the computer and therefore do not deal with parameters of the real, physical world. The few that are built are then confronted with these parameters. This event could be referred to as a process of translation, a process where the continuous elements and surfaces are subdivided into buildable ones.

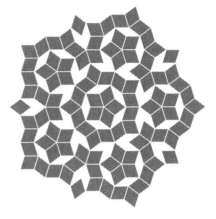

Although these translations are getting better and better, they are mostly treated as a bothersome necessity. One could say that the development of the software to create highly complex geometries has increased the discrepancy between architectural conception and realisation that was already existent before, giving rise to certain nicknames such as 'paper architects'.

TOP DOWN BOTTOM UP

But there is a chance to reunite the apparently contradictory attitudes and to reach the point where ambitious designs and buildability do not exclude each other anymore. One way of reuniting the two could be the approach of operative subdivision, which I would like to introduce here. The term operative subdivision looks like a contradiction in itself at first glance. The main reason for this might be that the meaning of the word subdivision is not usually used for processes that generate something but rather for processes applied to something already existent. It is in the logic of the word: in order to subdivide something one first needs something to divide. The notion of

'operative subdivision' is an attempt to introduce the idea that subdivision is not necessarily a mere post-creative operation. The opposite can be the case. It can be a device that influences the realisation of the final building.

A good example to illustrate how this could work on the level of CAAD, is a modelling technique that already exists, known as subdivision modelling. This technique uses a polygon model as its basis. However, this polygon model is not the final result but rather works as a skeleton. By applying subdivision, the jagged polygon skeleton is transformed into a smooth surface. The smoothness of this surface can be adjusted by changing the level

of subdivision. The basic polygon model stays relevant as its geometric constellation can still be changed by manipulating the control points. The interesting thing here is the fact that the application of subdivision creates something new by changing the condition of the starting object, in opposition to the usual usage of techniques like the 'Delaunay Triangulation' that is applied on computer generated curved surfaces in order to make them buildable.

On the subject of architectural design processes, one can already observe that the old 'top down' process is replaced by one that works 'bottom up'. Unit based design strategies are more and more often taught and applied at architectural schools. When talking of these current phenomena, it is impossible not to mention Gilles Deleuze and his influential book 'Difference and Repetition' as a reference. The student projects ask if it is possible to create a design with a certain starting unit, and if so, how. In this context, the principles of cellular automata or non-trivial patterns, like the Penrose pattern are studied. But even if the resulting designs are unitbased, often the question of how these units are built up stays unanswered. There is no relation to material or production parameters.

INTEGRATION

But why? Why not use the possibility to include material properties as design parameters? Why not take advantage of the full potential of computational design and integrate material aspects into the design process? Why not make the fact of the joint, resulting from material limitations, a part of the design process instead of implementing it afterwards? And finally, the notion of the whole and its parts could be extended beyond the material aspect towards the knowledge of the different disciplines. The combination of these in one coherent design process would result in a new level of inclusive architectural quality. The technology of today and of the future should be able to reunite the disciplines, as well as integrate the aspect of the unit or the necessary subdivision into software applications.

1) DAM, Deutsches Architekturmuseum Frankfurt am Main 2) '...Das Wort "Bauen" sollte aus dem Vokabular verschwinden und ersetzt werden durch ein Wort, das den Begriff der Montage beschreibt, des trockenen Fügens, das heißt die Kunst des Fügens oder besser "Die Kunst der Fuge". Das organische, logische System-Design wird dominieren.' Konrad Wachsmann Wendepunkt am Bauen

(UN)BOUNDED ON THE SOCIAL IN SPATIAL DESIGN PROCESSES

by gabi schillig

„ARCHITECTURE, SCULPTURE AND PAINTING ARE SPE-
CIFICALLY DEPENDENT ON SPACE, BOUND TO THE NE-
CESSITY OF CONTROLLING SPACE, EACH BY ITS OWN
APPROPIATE MEANS. THE ESSENTIAL THING THAT WILL
BE SAID HERE IS THAT THE RELEASE OF AESTHETIC
EMOTION IS A SPECIAL FUNCTION OF SPACE."

LE CORBUSIER, 1948 1)

choreographed geometry, spatial manipulation 6)

Space has the political tendency to close itself and architecture is the practice of organizing space. The employment of architectural knowledge is thus ideological and territorial, formed by a specific understanding of boundaries. On an urban scale, cities are the result of micro and macro conflicts played out each day in the political, economic and social realms. The space of conflicts has its own particular char- acteristics: topology, morphology, organisa-tion, rhythm and geometry.

Space is a medium of social relations, articu-lated as physical and symbolic distance, proximity, position, opposition and simultaneity. The production and control of space is thus crucial to any execution of power, representing its potency, reproducing its social order. Territorial conflicts are intensified through the systematic instrumentalisation of architecture and urban planning for the purpose of controlling space. In the context of the conflict in the Middle East, Eyal Weizman has written about *Destruction through Design* 2), as an essential component of urban planning and architecture, deployed as a weapon in urban warfare. Space acquires political meanings.

One of my arguments in this essay is that the social-political aspect of the organisation of space is not only manifest in existing housing and the urban fabric, but begins to germinate during the design process itself.

Spatial design strategies and the ambiguity of boundaries. Martina Löw argues in her book *Raumsoziologie* 3) that space constitutes itself as a social phenomenon within social processes. The user-subject becomes more important as social actor to define space through his or her ex-periences. The appropriation of space, but also its design and its representation become crucial in that sense. When thinking about space it is important to re-examine the notion of the bound-ary. Peter Marcuse writes about the ambiguous meaning of walls in his essay, Walls of Fear and Walls of Support 4) and asks "*Do walls provide security against attack, a protection of privacy? That depends*", he answers, "*not so much on the composition of the walls themselves, as on their social role.*" And he goes on: "*All walls are boundaries, but not all boundaries are walls.*" All of this calls into question the traditional role of boundaries. That role would seem to have expired, there is clearly a need for a new condition, a new process. Architecture has to redefine itself, its de-sign process and its political function.

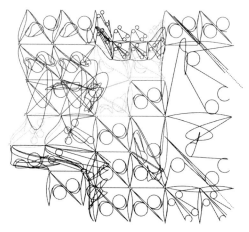

choreographed geometry, movement diagram 6)

So, what are innovative methods of spatial en-closure? Is there a new strategy needed for de-bordering space and how influential are innovative design methodologies? Spatial strategies have already been dealing with spatial continuums, the destruction of the box or the "*plan libre*". In each case a modern dynamic of diversity can be found and has been in each case the starting point for a new aesthetic space paradigm and the emergence of functional, ordered constructs.

Especially during the sixties, interventions in urban space and the contention of social spaces led to a different appreciation of space, reflected at the time in trans-disciplinary work in the visual arts, architecture, performance and film. Existing spatial conditions are a product of social power relations that are changeable and therefore subject to critique. Artistic actions connect sensual and haptic experiences of spatiality.

EXPERIMENTAL DESIGN STRATEGIES, APPLIED
SOCIAL AND EDUCATIONAL CONTEXTS

As soon as the design process as such, no matter on what scale, requires action, strategies and innovation within in a certain social, educational or professional setting, it is already a social act. The development of an idea is process-orientated and time-based. Within a social context the idea needs to be communicated by applying a certain "language" – whereby content is given a form which itself becomes again a carrier for content. The relationship between form and content is complex and needs a strategic argument where different dimensions and layers of each idea need to be defined. Within experimental design processes forms are temporal, constantly changing due to their ongoing negotiations with their surroundings. Experimental design is a method or set of actions and observations that offer diverse solutions to a particular question to support a hypothesis. The act of design is not ultimately framed by a singular aesthetic end, but by multiple constraints and ambitions of each project, as negotiated by the architect, designer and user. Within the field of *performative architecture* 5), for instance, architects construct private and public events, social situations and facilitate temporary spatial appropriation – architects become initiators of social processes and therefore construct social space.

Experimental design strategies and their spatial articulation of boundaries break down antiquated views and establish a three and four-dimensional space. Furthermore they enable, through critical interaction, discourse and its local context, the visualisation of social-political aspects of space. Multiple complexities of space and architecture cannot be condensed into a single formal criterion, but interrelational sets of criteria are needed to develop architecture through these emerging methods. A systematic logic of thought needs to be developed, mapping specific processes and requiring aesthetic sensibility and design ability.Systematically developed, spatial models are exposed to a number of manipulative processes that negotiate between different environments. Layered levels of design intelligence are required, incorporating organisational and spatial aspects, whereas repertoire and techniques are controlled through coordination, while precision can be achieved with specific techniques. Boundaries are understood in an ambivalent and critical state and blurred transitions are preferred to rigid definitions, creating atmospheres rather then areas. There is a redirection and randomisation of geometry into variations and options from which to choose. Aesthetic practice is a process that appears in design, appropriation and the formation of space. These spatial models are anti-hegemonic because they do not exclude different interpretations and allow for speculations. Art and architecture are practices through which aspects

choreographed geometry, participation 6)

of society and life may be challenged and re-negotiated both of them operate through ideas and reflections. During experimental design processes conditions need to be re-evaluated, value structures, and systems need constant critical analysis and engagement.

Engagement is experimental and spatial models have to be a point of departure for a critical, political and social examination in the field of architecture as an aesthetic practice. The production of architecture has to trigger critical engagement and introduce a sense of responsibility that allows the consideration of political and social consequences. The rad-icalisation of space and its design processes contribute toward a liberation from traditional values and thoughts. Conflicts force creativity. Inventive talent allows for new spatial conditions and appropriation of space improvisation becomes an important means within spatial design processes and a new kind of process-orientated definition of boundaries.

LITERATURE

1) Hartle, Johan: Der geöffnete Raum. Zur Politik der ästhetischen Form; Wilhelm Fink Verlag 2006

2) Weizman, Eyal: Räumliche Analysen der israelischen Siedlungspolitik; An Architektur Ausgabe zum Thema Krieg, Nr.6 Feb.2003 p.13

3) Löw, Martina: Raumsoziologie; Frankfurt am Main 2001

4) Marcuse, Peter: Walls of Fear and Walls of Support; in: Architecture of Fear, edited by Nan Ellin; Princeton Architectural Press 1997, p.101

5) see also: Knoess, Elke: Performative Architecture; in: Architektur Rausch – A Position on Architectural Design, edited by Thomas Arnold, Paul Grundei, Claire Karsenty; Jovis Verlag 2005

6) Choreographed Geometry; spatial installation by Gabi Schillig– developed during a fellowship at the Akademie Schloß Solitude Stuttgart, 2007 – The object consists of different geometric modules that form a programmed surface that allows users to interact and communicate, furthermore triggering mediation and new spatial and social conditions are created by the participants´ own body movements. The modulation of the body is disclosed by emphasizing its stimulus potential regardless of underlying ana-tomical conditions. It becomes provocative in appearance and new body constructs are moulded by the movement and interaction of participants within the garment. The garment itself becomes an interface between its users and their (built) surroundings – the body is being disembodied and space is being de-bordered. Controlling space becomes an important active instrument for the participants.

soft triangles

The original model structure was developed from an elastomer microstructure of synthetic material, consisting of long threads connected by flexible knotting points.

This spatial system was trans-lated into a triangular arrangement of connection points and their resulting surfaces. Geometrical events such as folding, overlapping, interweaving and cross-connecting were deployed to create spatial complexity and structural stability. The materiality of the metal surface intensifies spatial effects with its reflective properties.

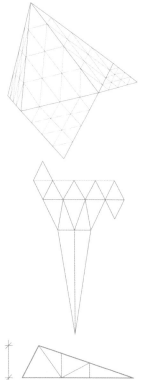

>TECHNIQUES triangulation, cutting, folding
>MATERIALS plastic threads, aluminium plate

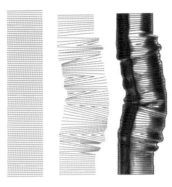

Using the technique of "hydro-forming", hollow metal bodies are forced into a negative form through the application of pressure. During this process, the metal body needs to be moved continuously by pistils. If their pressure is too high the system fails and a creased reject is produced.

This folding phenomena was investigated further by using felt material which is tested to the limits of its deformation in two axes. The higher the deformation and the instance of creasing, the higher its stability of surface.

multidirectional folding

>TECHNIQUES folding
>MATERIALS metal tube, felt

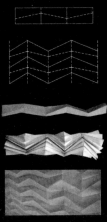

a folded wave structure, applied on
a piece of paper, allows credible
structural / organizational patterns
to emerge.

folded wave

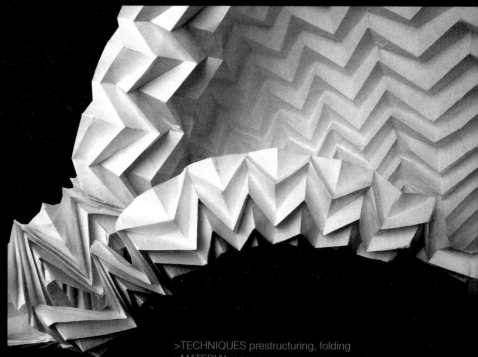

>TECHNIQUES prestructuring, folding
>MATERIAL paper

inversion

>TECHNIQUES prestructuring, folding
>MATERIAL paper

The starting point was a sheet of paper, which was pre-informed by subdividing it into equal smaller triangles. These triangles define the units and constraints for the main folding process that transforms the sheet into a spatial envelope. Thus the two-dimensional sheet is processed into a three-dimensional state.

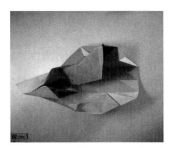

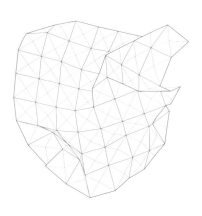

woven garment

A sheet of metallic mesh is being pre-informed by a fish bone folded pattern. The emerging hills and valleys are being filled with tyraps generating a woven garment.

>TECHNIQUES bending, knotting.
>MATERIALS aluminium mesh, tyraps

>TECHNIQUES knotting, looping, bending
>MATERIALS threads, metal wire

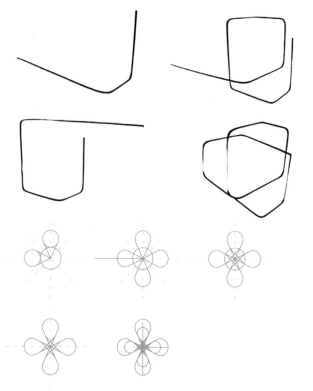

Knotting techniques are the basis of this modelling strategy. Knots are tight loops that form meshes when re-plicated. Furthermore they may be used to create different zones of density. The single modules were defined by the amount of bending moments and vary from open to closed knotting systems. Distributed in a field, different spatial zones and structural organisations arise.

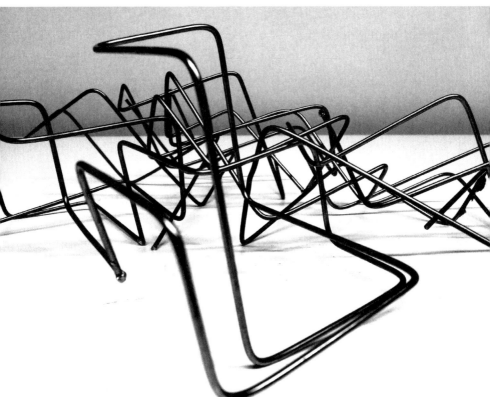

interlocking loops

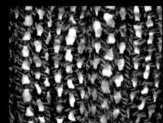

Various techniques and structures observed in textiles are taken as a starting point to explore spatial conditions. The result is a catalogue of geometries, surfaces and organisation patterns.

textile operations

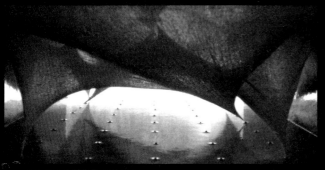

>TECHNIQUES weaving, bending, cutting, folding, layering
>MATERIAL paper, aluminium, cardboard, nylon

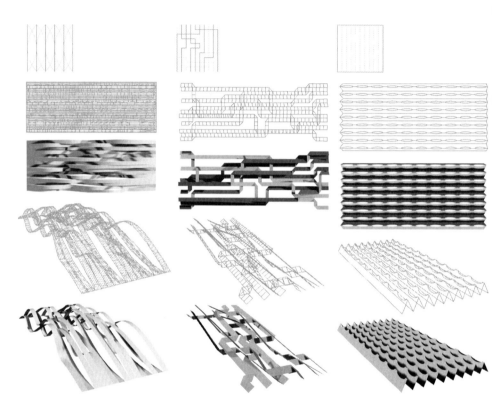

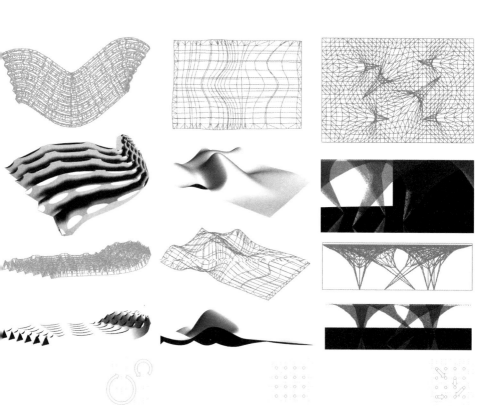

THE CONNECTION BETWEEN
CONCIOUSNESS AND MATTER
by maria blaisse

BY WATCHING EVOLUTION ONE REALIZES
THAT NATURE IS MAKING CHOICES ALL THE
TIME AND ADAPTING TO CHANGE. WE CAN
DO THE SAME

improvisation dive into the unknown
and experience the vast potential and
coherence of that moment

when working with a group of students
the qualities all together form a unity
when one is missing it is hard to continue

glimpses of the invisible give us a shift
in understanding processes in other
dimensions hard to understand with
our senses but very clear.

by being in contact with oneself and with the material you are working with. Then you see the full potential of the point where you are. There is a connection and coherence to the world around you that give access to a wider universe with more dimensions. Also to other disciplines like science, art, dance, music, philosophy. And from there one can carefully structure.

You are yourself a part of nature.

Then one can start using the computer.

The photographs show a travel through the form potential of a rubber inner tube which started in 1985. The process is still unfolding.

Right now I am working with flexible structures (deriving them from the spiral tube) and movement where there is a constant change of forms on bodyscale. Finally the form will rest in itself with all the possibilities incorporated.

This is the way of working towards architecture I am developing.

TAINTED LOVE INSTEAD OF ERASING THE FAULT, EMBRACE IT

by anja bramkamp

Daniel Heath, FH Nürnberg 2005

THE PHYSICAL MODEL SMELLS

Every design technique produces its own aesthetics which are represented in the product of a long term process. Many buildings tell us that they originated on a drawing board. The drawing board and 2D representations as the development drawing and 2D total elevation claim that they are the neutral view and representation of a building.

A neutral viewing point does not exist. The best approach to producing space is modelling, because space has at minimum 4 dimensions, x, y, z and time. These dimensions are only represented in a physical model. The physical model is always a defined scale in itself and in its constituent material. The access to the physical model is by movement. Instead the digital model is moving itself and asking the observer to stand still. In the phys-sical perception all the senses are required: smell, touch, sound and the visual. In the perception of the physical, each step towards the model increases our knowledge of the model. The physical model smells. The same concept adapts to different techniques and changes its appearance. Each individual technique has its own logic, dynamic and potential for error.

THE INTELLIGENCE OF THE FAULT

A fault allows a glimpse inside a system. The fault interrupts routines and questions the system as a whole. The Merriam-Webster dictionary defines a fault as a lack, like a deficit or a misdemeanour; something which differs from the standard. In the case of differing from the standard the definition of the value system which defines right or wrong has to be examined. A deficit must be examined where material properties are concerned.

The understanding of the beauty of a fault occurs to me in the work of Alison and Peter Smithson. Claude Lichtenstein and Thomas Schregenberger have this to say about their work 1) : *„AS FOUND is the tendency to deal with what is, to identify the existing, to follow its traces with interest: This interest relies on the experience that to acting like this allows for new insights and <forms> to arise, to be radically aware of something. The AS FOUND attitude is anti-utopic and the properties of the things they detect are direct, unmediated, rude and have a material presence."* Alison and Peter Smithson were part of the Independent Group founded in the mid fifties in Great Britain.

The Independent Group questioned the hegemonic idea of art as the opposite of the everyday. They considered art as arising from the everyday and popular culture, film and music. They questioned the heroic era of modern architecture which wanted to ease the living conditions of the masses by means of standardization. Rationalization and standard-ization carries a puritanical element. Control and function are the dominating themes. Alison and Peter Smithson intended an architecture which implied that 2) *„the pleasure of use is perfectly possible"*.

The task is to discover the poetry of the faults. To observe very carefully the process of modelling with all of the senses as well as the intellect. Faults are individuations. Any deviation from the standard creates something particular. To understand the quality of a fault means exploring the unknown and experimenting, being careful not to determine the result in advance but to cede control to the process of becoming.

MATERIAL TAKEOVER

At some point in the process of modelling in a clear setup the material should take command and the model maker should follow the constraints or possibilities of the material to the limit or even beyond the limits the material allows. Every step in this experiment must be documented and analysed. From the beginnings through to any deformations and the final self destruction.

It is an interplay between dominating the process and being dominated by the constraints of the material, understanding the logic of the materials behaviour and adapting this logic to integrate it into the design process. The aim is to discern the particular qualities of the materials, including even their faults. It should be possible to abstract the found qualities into a general context so that a translation into another material becomes possible. With wood for example, the particular qualities of the cracks creating a façade could be constructed in concrete or steel or plastics.

The physical model forces the transition from the immaterial to the material realm. Some consider the material world to be the point where the love story ends and the everyday begins-starts. As if an idea loses a lot of potential which relies on the blur effect, leaving plenty of space for speculation. But it is especially from everyday, as well as from various aspects of the materiality of physical models, that "an unlimited world of limited possibilities" can emerge. Because of moments when the routine is interrupted or the material is not doing what I might want it to do, an abudance of possibilities open up again and pursuing only one track is sabotaged. The realm of faults can then lead to new typologies to escape the unlimited repetition of the existing.

Stefan Müller, Mingh Ngyuen, FH Coburg 2007

LITERATURE
1) *AS FOUND Die Entdeckung des Gewöhnlichen Lars Müller Zürich, 2001*
2) *Alison and Peter Smithson, Changing the Art of Inhabitation, Artemis London, 1994*

PRODUCTION OF DIGITAL FORM

george katodrytis

DIGITAL UNCANNY

I would argue that from its inception, digital media were considered a discipline external to architecture. By definition the digital in architecture does not exist. Despite this, architecture seems to truly lend itself to digital exploration. It creates a topology of symbolic forms as digital constructs. More importantly, it manifests itself in the most ambiguous element – space – within which any projection moves freely and without fixed boundaries. The new technology of the digital media has managed to unravel the repressed condition and abandoned projects of 20th c architecture (Futurists and Surrealists), and to challenge the only ideology that created it: modernism and its associated technology. One may talk about the relationship between the digital uncanny and introjections.

In architectural terms, the search for modernism's repressed condition was concentrated in the domain that the modernists had clearly and polemically identified as the basis of their attack on tradition: the irrational, the decorative and the uncanny. A good example is Tzara's indictment of modern architecture as a "*complete negation of the image of the dwelling.*" "*Modern architecture,*" Tzara argued, "*as hygienic and stripped of ornaments as it wants to appear, has no chance of living...because it is the complete negation of the image of the dwelling.*"[2]

In the modernists' tradition, the line between nature and machine, between the organic and the inorganic seemed clear; organicism was a metaphor, not reality. But for the current digital media, the boundaries between organic and inorganic are blurred; the body itself, invaded and reshaped by technology, in turn invades and permeates the space outside, even as this space takes on dimensions that themselves confuse the inner an the outer, visually and physically. As Walter Benjiamin presciently observed, "*The work of Le Corbusier seems to arise when the 'house' as mythological configuration approaches its end.*"[3] Digital technology attempts to reincarnate these "mythological configurations," repressed by modernism, with the monstrous and anamorphic merging of animal and house as an oneiric machine, a machine for dreaming. After all, there is no architecture without dream, myth or fantasy.

The blurring of lines between the mental and physical, the organic and inorganic was transformed by the surrealists, especially Dali, into a formulation that stressed the intersection of the biological and the constructional, building and psyche, architecture and hysteria, in order to produce the ultimate object of desire, or its reification at least. Characterized by its mimesis of the digestible, it was an architecture that, in Dali's words "verified that urgent "function," so necessary for the amorous imagination: to be able in the most literal way possible to eat the object of desire." Walter Benjiamin stated that the intersection of technology and nature was represented by the displacement of symbols from Romanticism to Modernism.

Adorno's discussion of mimesis originates in a biological context in which mimicry (a mediator between life and death) is a zoological predecessor to mimesis.

Here we may begin to trace the affiliations of Surrealism and modernism on the level of technique - affiliates that were stated by Benjamin in the aphorism: "The reactionary attempt that seeks to detach the forms imposed by technique from their functional context and to make natural constants out of them – that is to say, to stylize them…" In Benjiamin's terms, the structure that unified the two was fetishism. For fetishism, in its multiple displacements, "suppresses the barriers which separate the organic from the inorganic world." It is as "*at home in a world of the inert as in the world of the modern mechanization of the dwelling in its mission of repression against the bric-a-brac of the nineteen century.*"[4]

MIMESIS

What happens, then, when the fusion between the organic and the inorganic takes form? Mimesis? A mimesis that has a multiple interpretation. Digital technology is mimicking architectural space so much that it becomes believable and "real," so that organic and inorganic matter, animate and inanimate forms become indistinguishable. Form becomes malleable and changeable and interactive, as though it imitates its occupants. The body fuses with its surroundings.

According to Walter Benjamin and Theodor Adorno's biologically determined model, mimesis is posited as an adaptive behavior that allows humans to make themselves similar to their surrounding environments through assimilation.[5] Through physical and bodily acts of mimesis (i.e. the chameleon blending in with its environment), the distinction between the self and other becomes porous and flexible. Rather than dominating nature, mimesis as mimicry opens up a tactile experience of the world in which the Cartesian coordinates of subject and object are not firm, but rather malleable.

Animals are seen as genealogically perfecting mimicry (adaptation to their surroundings with the intent to deceive or delude their pursuer) as a means of survival (figure 1). Survival, the attempt to guarantee life, is thus dependant upon the identification with something external. The manner in which mimesis is viewed, as a correlative behavior in which a subject actively engages in „*making oneself similar to an Other*", dissociates it from its definition as merely imitation.[6]

According to Adorno, "by means of the mimetic impulse, the living being equates himself with objects in his surroundings."7 This surely holds the key to exploring the question of how human beings situate themselves within their environment, and points to an area in which the domain of psychoanalysis may offer crucial insights into the mechanism by which humans relate to their habitat. It begins to suggest, for example, that the way in which humans progressively feel ‚at home' in a particular building, is through a process of symbolic identification with that building. They may come to identify with technological objects. This symbolic attachment is something that does not come into operation automatically; it occurs gradually.

Figure 1. The act of mimesis as a means for survival

Mimesis in Adorno, and in Walter Benjamin, is a psychoanalytic term - taken from Freud - that refers to a creative engagement with an object. Mimesis is a term, as Freud himself predicted, of great potential significance for aesthetics.

To understand the meaning of mimesis in Adorno we must recognize its origin in the process of modeling, of ‚making a copy of'. In essence it refers to an interpretative process that relates not just to the creation of a model, but also to the engagement with that model. In mimesis imagination is at work, and serves to reconcile the subject with the object. This imagination operates at the level of fantasy, which mediates between the unconscious and the conscious, dream and reality.

It is important to recognize here the question of temporality. Symbolic significance may shift, often dramatically, over a period of time. What was once shockingly alien may eventually appear reassuringly familiar. The way in which we engage with architecture must therefore be seen not as a static condition, but as a dynamic process.

Mimesis for Benjamin offers a way of finding meaning in the world, through the discovery of similarities. These similarities become absorbed and then rearticulated in language, no less than in dance or other art forms.

Architecture along with the other visual arts can therefore be viewed as a potential reservoir for the operation of mimesis. In the very design of buildings the architect may articulate the relational correspondence with the world that is embodied in the concept of mimesis. These forms may be interpreted in a similar fashion by those who experience the building, in that the mechanism by which human beings begin to feel at home in the built environment can also be seen as a mimetic one.

Mimesis, then, may help explain how we identify progressively with our surroundings. In effect, we read ourselves in our surroundings, without being fully conscious of it. "By means of the mimetic impulse," as Adorno comments, "the living being equates himself with objects in his surroundings." The aim throughout is to forge a creative relationship with our environment. When we see our values, reflected' in our surroundings, this feeds our narcissistic urge, and breaks down the subject/object divide. It is as though - to use Walter Benjamin's use of the term mimesis - in the flash of the mimetic moment, the fragmentary is recognized as part of the whole, and the individual is inserted within a harmonic totality. It is within the new digital spaces that the act of mimesis happens.[8]

ALGORITHMS AND THE BREEDING OF DIGITAL FORMS
One technique by which mimesis is be constructed is by Algorithms. Algorithms may be defined as a detailed sequence of procedures to solve a problem. As such algorithms may be programmed to execute a series of mimetic tasks. Genetic algorithms constitute a class of search algorithms especially suited to solving complex optimization problems. In addition to parametric optimization, genetic algorithms are used in creative design, such as combining components in a novel and inventive way and ultimately creating a new complexity of language and form. Genetic algorithms transpose the notions of evolution in nature to computers by imitating natural evolution (figure 3 and figure 4).

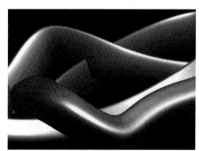
Figure 3. Evolutionary forms. Project by author

Figure 4. Algorithmic digital form.
Project by author

They find solutions to a problem by maintaining a population of possibilities according to the ‚survival of the fittest' principle. Because of this ability to "search" algorithmic scripts or codes generate form, which is precise and complex and which would be impossible to have conceived using the basic software interface and tools. Inevitably, a new universe of formal and compositional possibilities opens up and techniques for digital form-finding.

A common approach is to define a building envelope in terms of a series of parametrically defined elements such as the structural ribs. Some forms are curvilinear, non-planar and irregularly shaped, yet precise. Furthermore, some approaches that involve rule structures seek to generate designs via various forms of growth and/or repetition algorithms.

Additionally, there are approaches that seemingly abandon any kind of formal approach to shape generation but that seek to allow designers to "discover" meaningful shapes that exist within more complex geometrical patterns. Most of the approaches using formal shape-identification algorithms require specially written computational algorithms. Architects can now use advanced software to breed new forms rather than specifically design them. As De Landa notes, " … only if what results shocks or at least surprises, can genetic algorithms be considered useful visualization tools."[9]

Algorithms are based on non-linear wave function that through parametric differentiation organizers vectors of density. Can we then talk about fabricating of dense and large cityscapes, employing poly-directional structural networks?

On another level, the role of design has now been transformed into that of breeding fit and beautiful forms. There is clearly is an aesthetic component: the "sculpting" of beauty and the development of a personal artistic style. As with any socio-technological revolution throughout history, architecture inevitably invents a new formal language.

Ultimately, if traditional architectural representation has been based in resembling and describing the appearance of the architectural object, through its use the algorithm architectural notation has become operational; to design the choreographing of the transformation process. The architectural object is transformed into event and performance, either by understanding architecture as the dynamics of spatial conditions, or by the object being understood as the actualization of built-up potentials.

REFERENCES
1 VIDLER, A., 1996, The Panoramic Unconscious: Victor Burgin and Spatial Modernism, Essay introduction in Shadowed by Victor Burgin, Architectural Association, p.9.
2 TZARA, T., 1933, D''un certain automatisme du goût, Minotaure, 3-4, December, p. 84.
3 BENJIAMIN, W., 1982, Passagen-Werk, in Gesammelte Schiften, vol. 5 (Frankfurt: Suhrkamp), p. 513
4 BENJIAMIN W., 1930, Passagen-Werk, op. cit., p. 680, citing Salvador Dalí, 'L'âne pourri,' Surréalisme au service de la Révolution, I, pp. 693, 118
5 ADORNO, T., 1984, Aesthetic Theory, trans. C. Lenhardt (London: Routledge & Kegan Paul), p. 164
6 Ibid.
7 Ibid.
8 BENJAMIN, W., 1986. On the Mimetic Faculty, Reflections. New York: Schocken Books.
9 DE LANDA, M., 2001. Deleuze and the Use of the Generic Algorithmic in Architecture. Essay.

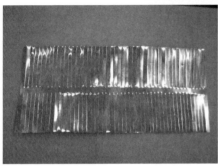

This model was generated by applying a folding technique to a planar surface. The emerging linear structure was then twisted, resulting in a form that resembles a spinal column.

The resulting tube-like geometry unfolds its linear substructures into space.

spinal spin

>TECHNIQUES cutting, cleaving, rotating, bending
>MATERIAL aluminium sheet

(a)symmetry

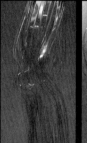

A transparent plastic tube is transformed into a circular, streaky model. Geometrical operations such as rotation, compression and thermoforming lead to a test series of deformations performed upon the tubular system. Symmetrical and asymmetrical deformations and layers are then materialized. Through the use of light projected on to the manipulated transparent tube, a variety of visual effects were produced. Zones of different light densities were created, suggesting further possibilities and uses.

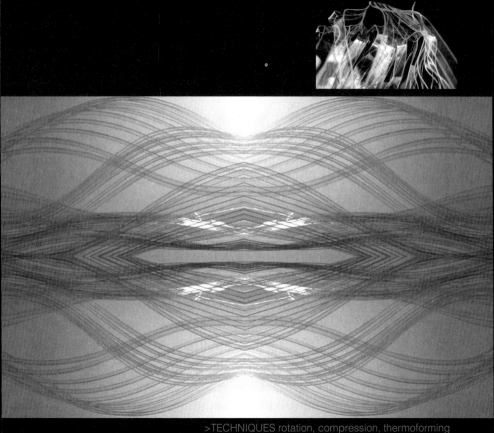

>TECHNIQUES rotation, compression, thermoforming

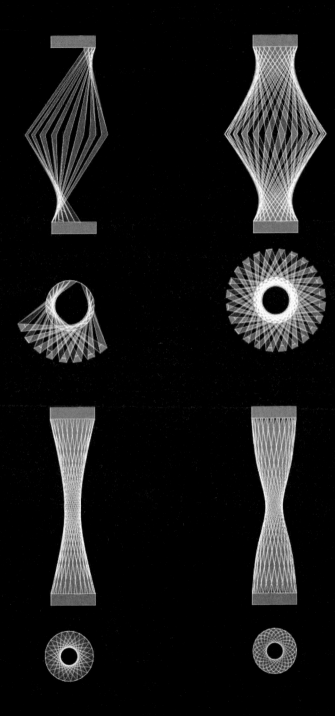

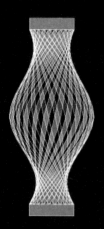

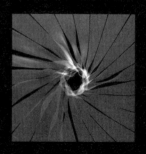

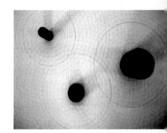

>TECHNIQUES cutting, bending
>MATERIAL cardboard

cause and effect

Several attractors are placed on a virtual surface. They generate concentric wavelike movements and deformations, both horizontally and vertically. The surface unfolds its spatial potential, and cause and effect become inseparable in the resulting model.

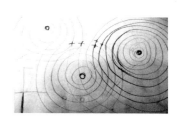

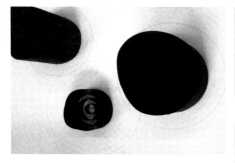

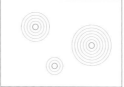

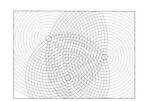

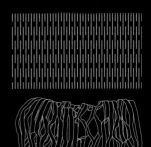

A linear grid is being applied on a planar surface, allowing it to deform and react to different conditions.

Next, various section profiles are generated by forming the surface into a cylinder, providing rigidity and stability at the same time. The construction becomes a skin.

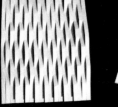 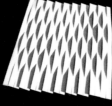

>TECHNIQUES cutting, bending, thermoforming
>MATERIAL cardboard, pvc

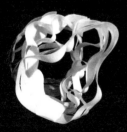

linear surface

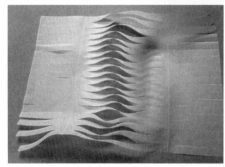

A piece of paper is cut following a linear pattern on both of its shorter sides, resulting in a set of stripes that meet in the middle zone. At this point, the ends of the stripes were moved in both planar directions, creating an interwoven topography.

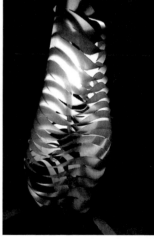

interwoven stripes

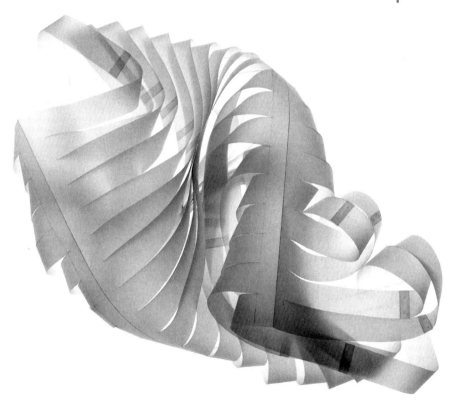

>TECHNIQUES cutting, bending, folding
>MATERIAL cardboard, paper

Four hexagonal units, with differing angles and side lengths offer multiple variations when replicated, thus creating different cluster modules. The undulating comb surface this produces can be read as a skin, structure, floor plan, section or urban plan. Nevertheless, it is a puzzle of indefinite geometries.

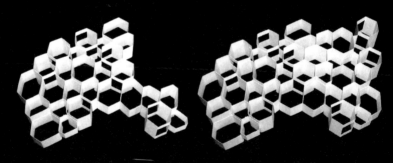

increasing clusters

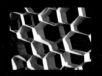

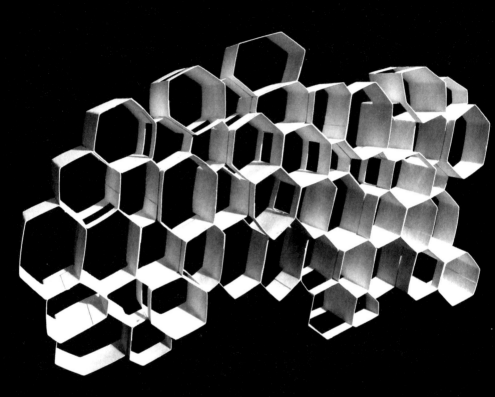

>TECHNIQUES folding, multiplying
>MATERIALS cardboard

transformative knot

>TECHNIQUES indenting, punching, bending, multiplication
>MATERIALS cardboard, acrylic paint, acrylic glass

The Y shape was chosen as a modular element, originally derived from patterns observed in a fingerprint. In order to ensure a three-dimensional outcome, the Y shapes were geometrically bent along different axes. One entity consists of up to five modules, where each module links to two other elements. A dynamic knot is being generated.

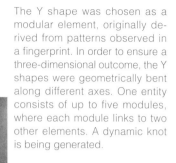

Due to their flexibility of movement, a variety of different spatial configurations could be formed. The degree of flexibility is defined by the material and its cross section: the greater the thickness of the material, the more constrained any movement becomes. The knot acts both as a structural and a spatial device.

 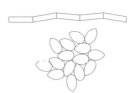 

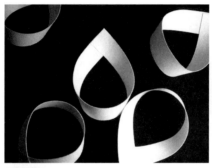 

This project is based on the idea of a growing organism. It is composed of modular loops in different dimensions, which are repeated and rotated by 180°.

The resulting cluster operates as a three-dimensional irregular grid, offering spatial variety on a micro or macro scale. The model can be read as an organisational pattern, a structural system or a surface condition.

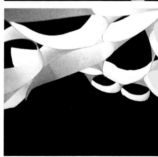

>TECHNIQUES cutting, bending, multiplying, rotating

>MATERIAL cardboard

iterative growth

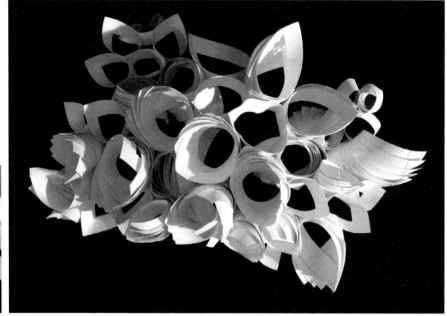

rhombus³

 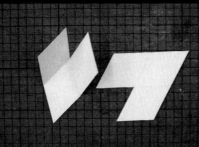 

Two linear elements are joined to create a rhombic module which can be positioned at different angles. The embedded building mechanism allows the collection of modules to form a cluster which adopts all the characteristics of the single unit: linear spatial transformability.

>TECHNIQUES cutting, folding, adding, evolving

>MATERIAL cardboard

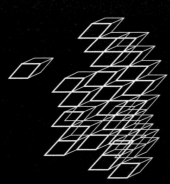

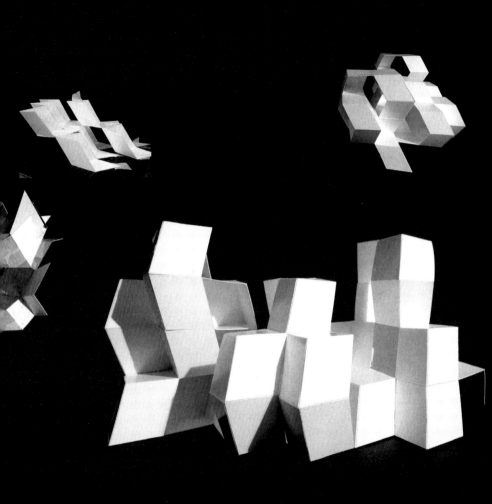

A GENERIC SOMETHING

by michael schwarz

Beyond a doubt the use of digital technology in architecture led to a simplification of workflow, especially in the pragmatic execution of an elaborated design. On the other hand these developments also led to an absence of identification and readability. By dealing intensively with these programs, not with the architecture that it creates, the intellectual design-approach concentrates on a process of form finding, based on the particular capabilities of this animation software. Per se this must not be of poor quality, but the use of a formal approach also needs the background of an overall conceptual strategy to strengthen the project. The partial loss of this approach can not only be be explained by the fascination of digital media and technique exerts on the user, it is also a case of a political and social change in the society, whereby the individual is educated with a lack of discriminatory powers.

Near the end of the eighties, a development occurred in the western world, which gave priority to the individualization of the individual. This process was supported by the governments then in power, with all available means. By creating the new value of personal uniqueness, the integration of the individual into a system could be ensured and the assimilation into a social grouping which stood beyond political and social control could be prevented An important result of this relationship, which was successfully reached, was a turn towards material values that were detrimental to social and humanistic ideals. This development was supported by a media industry which sent their main figures, good looking and equipped with the needy accessories, via TV series like "Miami Vice" into the houses of the people. It was no longer a matter of content. Content was subordinated to superficial structures like fashion, accessories, cars and so on. Henceforth appearance and not being dominated the personal awareness of a generation growing up. The by-product to was the questioning of a definition of capitalism by Karl Marx, who described capitalism as a class society. As soon as the proletariat does not have the feeling, that the accumulation of social wealth is at their own expense, the perception of a two-class-society will vanish and a third class will be established. Traditional class interests will change, and the problem will shift downwards. Exactly this happened.

These changes affected creative processes as well, as we can see it inter alia in architecture. The scenario described above leads to a superficial view of architecture and space, in which the conceptual debate does not happen anymore. As a result we can observe an interchangeability of projects and their design. Only a few architects worldwide attempt to apply a conceptual approach to the project, which then develops structure and form. Unfortunately, not at least due to the influence of the worldwide media-industry, these results get copied and show up somewhere else. One cannot fail to note, that these projects often have a quality of style, which is not based on inherent design-procedures, but on the use of digital technique and the effects coherent with those. That way formal objects appear, which add to the theory of the "Iconic Building" a new meaning. If one declares this to be another crisis in architecture, this would not be house made, but the result of a development of society, which architects are reluctant to criticize. Critique always means dispute, and the ability for this seems to be aborted.

If one considers the work of students, it is easy to find out, that these young architects in general use similar approaches worldwide. The work is more or less interchangeable. If it was it possible in the past to recognize the the work of the universities and academies, it is nowadays nearly out of any question. As a prerequisite the lowest common denominator is the mastery of digital programs like 3D-Studio Max, Rhinoceros or Maya.

Against this background it will be interesting to observe, how the identity of the building and identification with the urban situation will evolve. There is the chance, that if we take the globalization-process into consideration, there will be an identification with the condition, less with a place. The needful intellectual discussion could lead to a highly interesting conceptual approach for buildings and architecture, which would shows projects producing an immaterial transparency. This transparency then has to be changed into materiality without any hierarchy of approaches of design or procedure. A generic something.

THE IMPORTANCE OF MODELLING

by yves weinand

THE CONCEPTUAL REVIVAL OF SO-CALLED DYNAMIC ARCHITECTURE

Architecture is these days still considered by the general public as something stable, immobile or definitive. However, architecture is inhabited by lives; it is at its best living, and it integrates dynamic systems. Untill now, architecture has been unaware of the dynamic proprieties inherent in it. New trends in contemporary architectural research demonstrate that the static reference points in place to date have been replaced by dynamic reference points. The notions of "flow", "movement" and "fluidity" are associated with architectural design. Links are created connecting technological notions from the world of science to formal and aesthetic notions from the world of art. Architects today seek inspiration in other areas or disciplines: fluid dynamics, the simulation of traffic flows, rheology (composite materials for example), mineralogy, medicine, biology and even geology and rock mechanics.

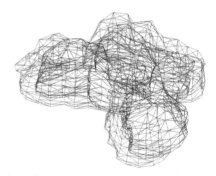

Sarah Coenes, computer-generated wire-frame model (Atelier Weinand EPFL)

But these disciplines are rarely understood on a microscopic scale, and when they are indeed interpreted on the scale of an architectural production, a shortfall is apparent. One can, however, observe that the interprtations of scientific knowledge used in the dis-cipline of architecture are limited to the simple immediate visual interpretation of these technical and physical phenomena. An innovative approach consists in including the various levels of interpretation and understanding as a whole by allowing for a double visual/aesthetic and scientific/analytical reading.

IMPORTANCE OF MODELLING
The approach presented is based on producing models, and more particularly on learning how to produce them. Making virtual and physical models allows the objectives cited in the introduction to be achieved.

The model designer positions himself as a builder. This point of view bestows upon the person and the object a double identity: firstly an artisan identity in the sense stipulated by the Werkbund (cf. the "neue Sachlichkeit" (new objectivity) from the beginning of the last century), then an interdisciplinary identity which allows for the professions of architect, engineer, acoustician and others to be coordinated. The homogenisation of artistic and scientific considerations is achieved by making models in real time. The various adaptations made through the course of the evolution of the model are also made in real time. The traditional dichotomy separating art and science is thus approached not through an intellectual dialogue, but by making virtual and physical models.

The role of the model consists in creating a link between architecture and structural aspects, between art and science. The new phenomena mentioned in the introduction, which consist of integrating scientific notions when defining an architectural concept, are conveyed by making models. Technological and formal notions are interconnected. The notions of movement, flow and generation are integrated into the creative processes and linked to the notions of architectural design.

It is important to make this approach, which has taken off in an academic context, a reality through physical production. Indeed, the files used allow the line of data transmission to be extended up to the actual production of the elements of walls and roofing or even structural elements. Demonstrating the actual constructability of these architectures is the aim of making various prototypes of different scales developed right up to their constructive details.

Sarah Coenes, computer-generated wire-frame model (Atelier Weinand EPFL)

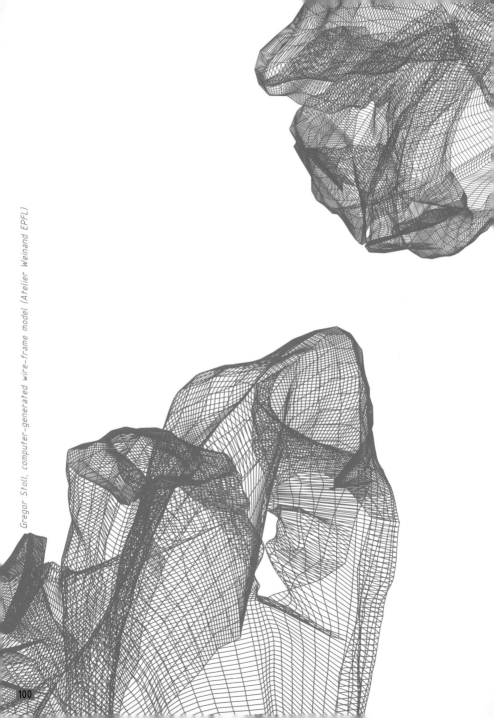

Gregor Stoll, computer-generated wire-frame model (Atelier Weinand EPFL)

DREAM AND REALITIES, ON-SCREEN IMPRESSIONS
The clarity of the line on screen. The trompe l'œil of a perception that is "warped" on screen. And then, the strength of the physical world. The model serves as a way, a mediator, of transporting a vision – the dream – and projecting it into reality; and of checking it. Abandon the utopia that consists in believing that everything can be foreseeable. Allow us to discover step-by-step, and readjust afterwards. Progress does not lie in the verb, that is to say in the ability of the architect to infer a priori, but instead in a parallel lucidity, that is intuitive and humble. One is an artisan/designer and not a utopian visionary. One has one's feet on the ground, but one's head in the clouds.

These texts were first published in the book 'New Modeling' by Yves Weinand.

synbot

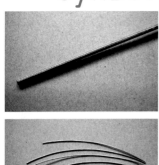

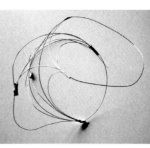

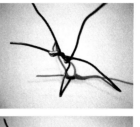

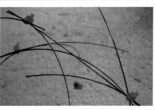

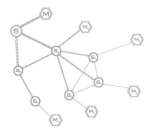

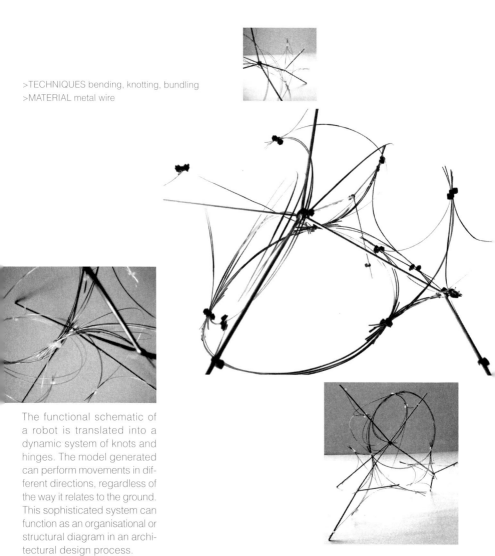

>TECHNIQUES bending, knotting, bundling
>MATERIAL metal wire

The functional schematic of a robot is translated into a dynamic system of knots and hinges. The model generated can perform movements in different directions, regardless of the way it relates to the ground. This sophisticated system can function as an organisational or structural diagram in an architectural design process.

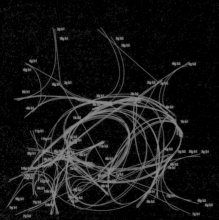

multiple perspective

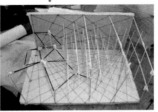

Playing games with perspective, this project is more than just a three-dimensional articulation of a triangulated surface. Perspective drawings build up the base for the three-dimensional matrix upon which that surface is built.

There is one horizontal and one vertical sheet, each furnished with a perspective drawing. They are arranged in an L shape. On the intersecting points of each drawing, vertical wooden profiles were placed. The points where the vertical and horizontal lines meet are the points upon which the surface is mapped.

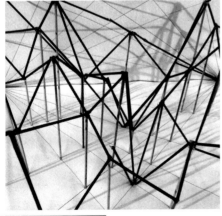

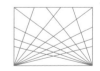

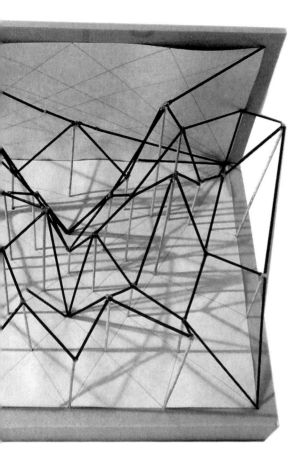

>TECHNIQUES cutting, connecting
>MATERIALS wooden sticks

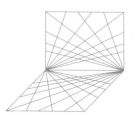

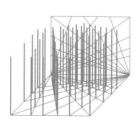

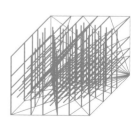

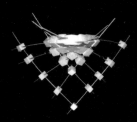

>TECHNIQUES cutting, knotting
>MATERIALS wooden sticks, styrofoam

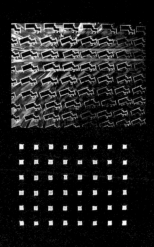

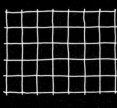

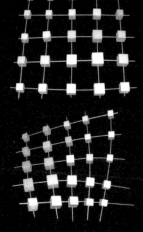

A linear rectangular grid is taken as a starting point to create a dynamic mesh which is able to generate infinite types of spatial conditions.

The different sizes of the knots intensify the spatial distortion of the emerging surface. The model is made from linear beams joined together by cubic knots, varying in size.

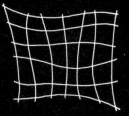

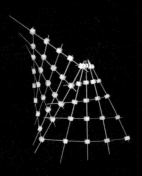

space matrix

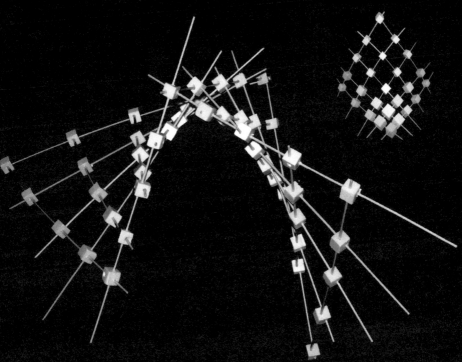

Two irregular comb grid systems are connected with a nylon membrane. The material properties of the membrane operate as a spatial generator. Pillars are formed organically between the two planes, resulting in a structural container that carries embedded spatial units, recalling the sculptural work of artist Ernesto Neto.

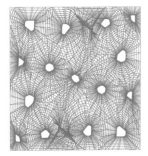

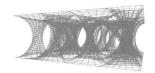

comb connection

>TECHNIQUES cutting, sewing, bending, stretching
>MATERIAL nylon membrane, PVC

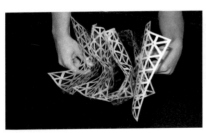

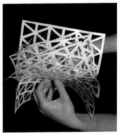

>TECHNIQUES cutting, folding, adding.
>MATERIAL pvc sheets

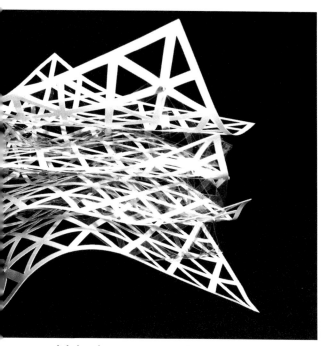

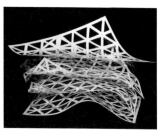

multi-layered surfaces

A number of self similar surfaces are being perforated in a rhombic pattern. They are later being accumulated on top of each other and fixed in their centre, creating a performative multi- layered surface.

asterios agkathidis

Born 1974 in Thessaloniki, Greece. Asterios Agkathidis studied architecture in the Aristotle university of Thessaloniki and the RWTH Aachen, completing his postgraduate studies in Advanced Architectural Design at the Staedelschule, Frankfurt in 2001. He became a partner in the architectural practice b&k+ in Cologne until 2004, then at VMX architects, Amsterdam until 2005. He later founded the architecture and research laboratory a3lab Frankfurt-Thessaloniki. Teaching and lecturing experiences include adbk Nuremberg, TU Darmstadt, the University of Thessaloniki, the FH Bielefeld, the Islamic University Malaysia the Städelschule and the Lebanese American University as visiting assistant professor.

markus hudert

Born in 1974. Markus Hudert studied architecture at the University of Applied Sciences in Coburg and at the Städelschule, Frankfurt, completing his postgraduate diploma there in 2002. From 2003 to 2006 he lived in the Netherlands, where he worked for the internationally renowned architectural offices UN Studio Van Berkel and Bos and Benthem Crouwel Architekten. He lectured and taught at the TU Darmstadt and at the University of Applied Sciences in Coburg. Since 2006 he has been a scientific collaborator at EPFL in Lausanne, where he is currently working on his PhD.

gabi schillig

Born in 1977. Gabi Schillig studied architecture at the University of Applied Sciences Coburg and Conceptual Design at the Städelschule. She has worked for several architectural offices, including Harry Seidler & Associates (Sydney), Architectural Studio Daniel Libeskind (Berlin) and Architekturbüro [lu:p] (Coburg). From 2005 to 2007 she was Academic Assistant at the Städelschule Architecture Class. She has been a visiting lecturer at the University of Innsbruck, TU Darmstadt, ABK Stuttgart, FH Coburg, FH Nuremberg and the International Summer Academy Salzburg. She has received grants from the Carl-Duisberg Society (2000), the Bavarian State Ministry for Research, Science and the Arts (2002-2004) and the Award for Young Emerging Artists by the City of Coburg 2007. Since April 2007 she has been a fellow of the Akademie Schloß Solitude in Stuttgart. Since October 2007 she has been teaching at the Berlin University of the Arts.

johan bettum

Born in 1962. Johan Bettum studied architecture at the Architectural Association in London after getting a BA. with a major in biology from Princeton University. He has taught, amongst other institutions, at the Architectural Association, UCLA and the EPFL in Lausanne and lectured and published widely on materials, design geometry and advanced digital modelling. From 1998-2002, he was a research fellow in Oslo where he ran a nationally funded research project on polymer composite materials in architecture. He was a member of the international design group OCEAN from 1996-2000. While maintaining a small practice, ArchiGlobe, devoted to experiments and research, Johan is currently completing his doctoral thesis on polymer composites in architecture. The thesis is an attempt at a revision of tectonic theory as well as a deliberation on the practical aspects that arise in architectural design when using these materials. Johan Bettum is the Programme Director of the Städelschule Architecture Class in Frankfurt am Main.

maria blaisse

Born in 1944. She studied textile design at the Gerrit Rietveld Academy in Amsterdam. She was a trainee in Jack Lenor Larsen´s design studio in New York. Later she researched traditions of textile-making and natural dyeing of fibres in South America. 1974-1987 she taught textile and flexible design at the Gerrit Rietveld Academy. In 1987 she designed hats for the Issey Miyake collection, shown in Paris and Tokyo. She has designed costumes for theatre and dance performances and has participated in major exhibitions of jewellery and textile design, including the Biennales in Lausanne, Paris and Kyoto. Maria Blaisse has lectured on the development of fashion and design at many symposia and workshops and has been guest lecturer at international academies, including Geneva, Berkeley, Hamburg, Kassel, Utrecht. In 2000, 2001 and 2007 she directed the class "Finding Form" at the International Summer Academy in Salzburg. She lives and works in Amsterdam.

anja bramkamp

Born 1966. Anja Bramkamp studied history and political science at the University of Cologne for two years and later continued her studies in architecture at the University of Applied Sciences Nuremberg. She gathered working experience as a carpenter and as a practicing architect in the architectural office Stößlein Harlé Architekten in Nuremberg, later starting her postgraduate studies in Advanced Architectural Design at the Städelschule in Frankfurt, graduating in 2004. Since then she has been running her own architectural practice "studio b" in Nuremberg. She also holds teaching positions in Nuremberg and Coburg and writes for the German online architectural magazine Baunetz.

george katodrytis

B.A.(Hons), A.A. Dip., R.I.B.A. An architect involved in practice, teaching and research. He is currently Associate Professor at the American University of Sharjah, U.A.E. He studied and taught architecture at the Architectural Association in London and he has lectured and exhibited extensively. He has worked in Paris, London, Nicosia and Dubai. His current work addresses issues of contemporary architecture, urbanism and cultural theory, with a focus on design, digital experimentation and writings on the contemporary 'city' as it is evolving in the 21st century.

michael schwarz

Born in 1958. After graduating at the University of Applied Sciences Darmstadt, he applied for the Master class of Peter Cook at the Staedelschule Frankfurt, which he finished in 1991. From 1991 to 2000 Michael was an associated partner in "Schwarz + Witthoeft architects" in Mannheim and Dresden and had his own practice from 2000 / 2004 with his wife, "Schwarz and Funke architects" in Heidelberg. In 2005 he started teaching as a visiting professor at the American University Sharjah (VAE). Since 2006 he has been a full faculty member at the Ajman University of Science and Technology in Ajman and a visiting professor at the Iranian University in Dubai. Michael Schwarz runs the think tank "starwalls" since 2005. He lives and works in Dubai.

yves weinand

Born in 1963. Yves Weinand studied Civil Engineering at the Ecole Polytechnique Fédérale de Lausanne EPFL after getting a degree in architecture from the Institut Supérieur d'Architecture Saint-Luc in Liège. In 1998 he received his PhD in applied sciences from the RWTH Aachen. In 1996 the Bureau d'études Weinand was founded in Liège, Belgium. Since 2004 he has been director of the Laboratory of Timber Construction at the EPFL Lausanne.

CREDITS

edititors
asterios agkathidis
markus hudert
gabi schillig

authors
asterios agkathidis
markus hudert
gabi schillig
+
johan bettum
maria blaisse
anja bramkamp
george katodrytis
michael schwarz
yves weinand

proof reading
geoffrey steinherz
iori wallace

photo credits
asterios agkathidis
andrea jäger
lars müller
bodil nordmeyer
gabi schillig

design
asterios agkathidis
markus hudert
gabi schillig

printed and bound
Druckhaus Berlin-Mitte

ISBN
978 3 8030 0746 9
third print

information

www.a3lab.org / mail@a3lab.org
www.markushudert.com / info@markushudert.com
www.gabischillig.de / info@gabischillig.de

Sole Distributor in the United States of America and Canada:
D.A.P./Distributed Art Publishers,155 6th Avenue, 2nd Floor
New York, NY 10013, U.S.A. www.artbook.com

our special thanks to

the fg_ekon, akademie schloß solitude stuttgart, criss yetzios from formZ, Sasa Lada, Aleka Alexopoulou, Rolf Eckstein and all contributors.